DISCOVER MY WORLD

Ocean

Written by Ron Hirschi
Illustrated by Barbara Bash

A BANTAM LITTLE ROOSTER BOOK
NEW YORK · TORONTO · LONDON · SYDNEY · AUCKLAND

OCEAN

A Bantam Little Rooster Book / September 1991

Little Rooster is a trademark of Bantam Books, a division of
Bantam Doubleday Dell Publishing Group, Inc.
All rights reserved.
Copyright © 1991 by Ron Hirschi.
Illustrations copyright © 1991 by Barbara Bash.

Calligraphy by Barbara Bash

Library of Congress Cataloging-in-Publication Data
Hirschi, Ron.
    Ocean / by Ron Hirschi ; illustrated by Barbara Bash.
        p.   cm. — (Discover my world)
    Summary: Various ocean animals describe their own behavior and
physical characteristics and ask the reader to guess what they are.
    ISBN 0-553-07470-9. — ISBN 0-553-35214-8 (pbk.)
    1. Marine fauna—Juvenile literature.   [1. Marine animals.
2. Literary recreations.]   I. Bash, Barbara, ill.   II. Title.
III. Series: Hirschi, Ron. Discover my world.
QL122.2.H57   1991
591.92—dc20   90-31817
                                                          CIP
                                                          AC
Published simultaneously in the United States and Canada

Bantam Books are published by Bantam Books, a division of
Bantam Doubleday Dell Publishing Group, Inc. Its trademark,
consisting of the words "Bantam Books" and the portrayal of
a rooster, is Registered in U.S. Patent and Trademark Office
and in other countries. Marca Registrada. Bantam Books, 666
Fifth Avenue, New York, New York 10103.

PRINTED IN HONG KONG

0 9 8 7 6 5 4 3 2 1

For my special friend, Daniel
—R.H.

To Wiley Basho
—B.B.

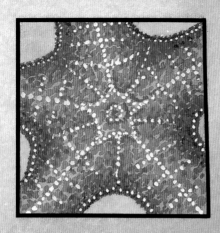

Down deep beneath the waves
where tides wash the silver sand,
starfish crawl along the ocean floor.
Who swims past the waiting arms
of these many-colored stars
in their home at the bottom
of the sea?

Who am I,
sharp teeth menacing every fish,
big and small?

Who hides beneath
the shimmering ribbons of kelp,
slipping in to hide,
slithering out to seek?

And who casts a wide-winged
shadow across the ocean floor?

I click and snap my two strong claws when the skate's shadowy shape slips past.

Can you guess our name?
We swim in silver swirling schools.
Our eyes glisten like
sparkling jewels.

Who am I?
I wear a tiger's stripes
and swim with quick, strong
strokes of my fan-shaped tail.

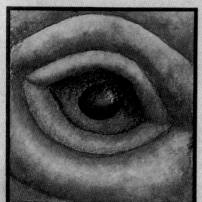

Weeeeoop!
Oooooohp! Ooooooooohp!
Who sings this mysterious song?
Could this be the greatest creature
on land or sea?

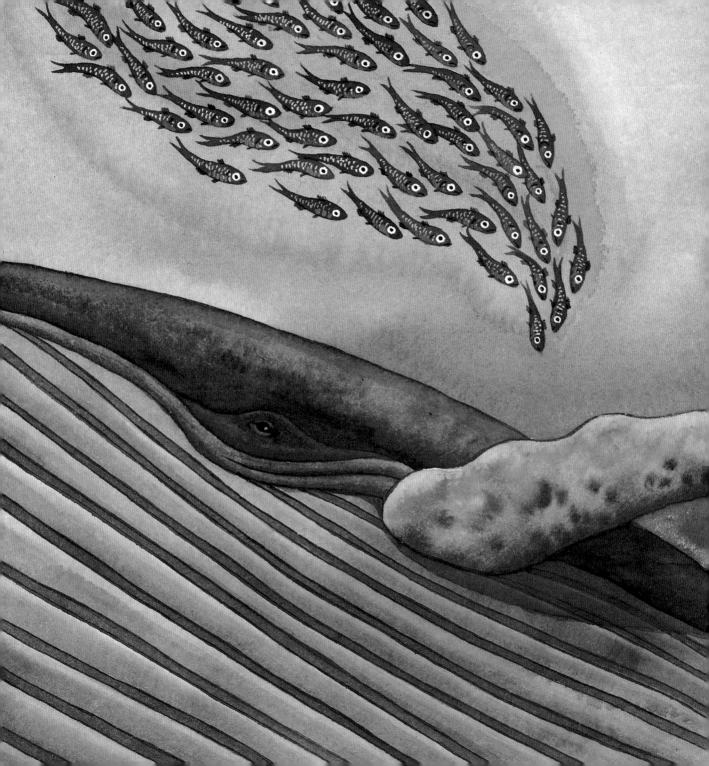

Do you know my name?
I swim on my back while I crack
my fresh clam dinner.

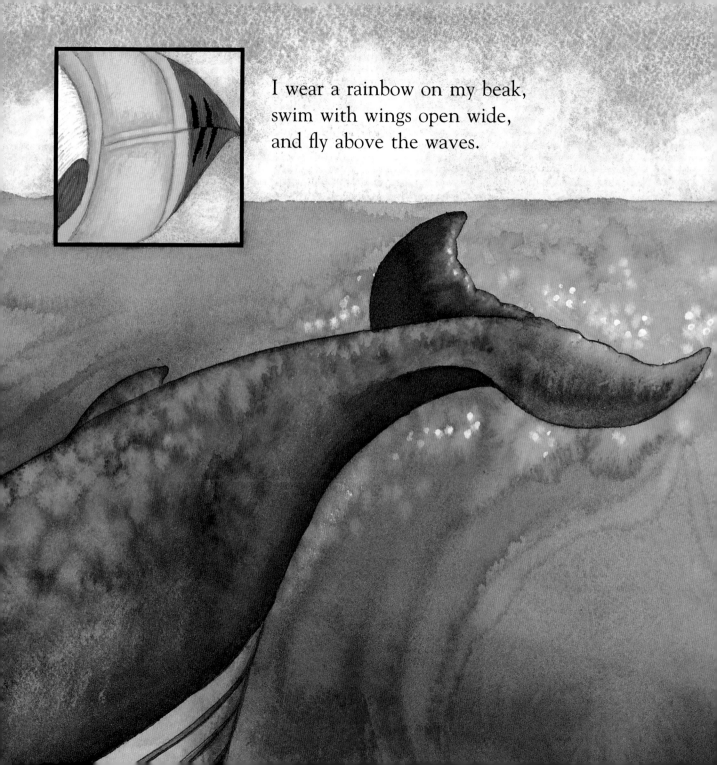

I wear a rainbow on my beak,
swim with wings open wide,
and fly above the waves.

Who am I?
Slicing past the puffin island
and leaping high into the air,
I breathe, just like you.

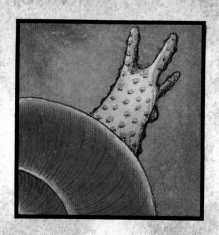

I can crawl,
and I can hide
my slender spiral
where sea meets land.

Who reaches down
to hold this tiny snail
in his gentle hand?

 Starfish trap clams, snails, and mussels by holding tight with tentacles that cover the underside of each long leg. They drill through a clam's hard shell with their chisellike mouthparts.

 Sharks could not survive without their sharp teeth. The blue shark comes equipped with spares. Growing in rows, its teeth are replaced as old ones break or wear out.

 Crab claws are hard because crabs wear their skeletons on the outside of their bodies. As a crab grows, it sheds this outer shell, revealing a larger body complete with a new set of snapping claws.

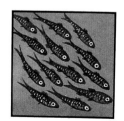 Like many tiny animals, the herring finds safety in numbers. These silver-scaled fish swim together in large groups called schools. Individual fish are safer in the school than out on their own.

Ocean Discoveries

 Many types of eels swim the seas and some kinds spend time in fresh water. All eels have long, slender bodies specially adapted to fit into tight places where they wait in ambush or hide from enemies.

 Fish come in many unique shapes. A skate's wide, flat body helps it to hide on the ocean floor. Using winglike fins, it glides through the sea much like an eagle soaring on the wind.

 Vertical stripes help hide angelfish among the reefs and also hide their eyes, making it difficult for predators to know which way these fish will flee—is it heads or tails?

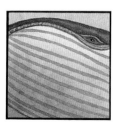 A humpback whale's song can be as short as a few minutes or as long as half an hour. The whale may repeat the same song for several hours at a time. The voices of some whales can travel as far as one hundred miles.

 Sea otters scratch and groom themselves by using their claws like a comb. This allows air bubbles to collect in their thick fur. These air bubbles help the otters keep warm and stay afloat as they eat or sleep.

 A puffin's wings are adapted to a seagoing life. They are short and strong enough to act as swim fins underwater, yet long and wide enough to lift the puffin above the waves and into the air.

 Porpoises breathe air, just like you. As mammals, they also nurse their young. Curious and intelligent, the porpoise speaks a language all its own, with sounds produced by releasing air through its blowhole.

 Snails' shells are beautiful to look at and protect the snail from pounding surf and predators. Empty shells are a welcome home for other sea life, helping hermit crabs and tiny fish survive into the future.